Never Pass Up an Opportunity

Larry Czerwonka

May your life be filled with amazing opportunities with aloha

Larry

The Larry Czerwonka Company
Hawaii

DEDICATION

For my Mom who brought me nothing but opportunities and possibilities when I was growing up and who spent more hours than I can ever repay in a single lifetime reading with me and playing with army men on the floor or "grocery store." She always let me know that there was never a limit as to what I could do with my life and she always believed in my potential.

ABOUT THE COVER

The cover photograph was taken by Sebastian P. Saarloos on the Big Island of Hawaii on January 12, 2012. Sebastian is an amazing photographer who lives and works in Alaska. You can view more of his photographs at http://www.facebook.com/SebastianSaarloos

CONTENTS

#18	help others to **SUCCEED**
#19	turn a frown into a **SMILE**
#20	take a day off and **RECHARGE**, especially if you can do it outdoors!
#21	**HELP** someone else step into the spotlight
#22	**IMPROVE** yourself
#23	leave a place **BETTER OFF** than you found it
#24	**SPEND TIME** with family and friends
#25	**TRY SOMETHING** you have never done before
#26	grow a **SMILE** on someone's face :)
#27	**ENCOURAGE** someone to pursue their dreams
#28	have a **GOOD TIME**!
#29	be curious, excited and **ENGAGED** with life
#30	start a **NEW TRADITION**
#31	**LEARN** to say 'hello,' 'thank you' and 'pardon me' in another language
#32	create **PEACE** in your life
#33	weave something **NEW** into the tapestry of your life
#34	live by the words you **SPEAK**
#35	**REINVENT** your life
#36	ask yourself "**WHAT** am I trying to do with my life?"
#37	keep **MOVING** forward
#38	be **OVER THE TOP**

#39   **ASSOCIATE** yourself with passionate and caring people

#40   associate yourself with slightly **CRAZY** people

#41   get off the beaten path and **EXPLORE** the road less traveled

#42   **CHANGE** the question

#43   see someone not as they are today but as what they might **BECOME**

#44   step back and **APPRECIATE** what you just created

#45   remain **FOCUSED** on your destination

#46   **SPEAK ENTHUSIASTICALLY**, to motivate and inspire others

#47   **GET ALONG** with others

#48   help a caterpillar become a **BUTTERFLY**

#49   picture Your **SUCCESS**

#50   do things that **BLOW PEOPLE AWAY** in their scope and uniqueness

#51   do things that **INSPIRE** others

INTRODUCTION

Each day, if we are paying attention, we are presented with a multitude of opportunities the problem is that quite often we are too "busy" to notice them.

You see, I do not believe in chance or fate or the "law of attraction." If chance or fate or the law of attraction really existed then all we'd have to do to be successful is sit and wait for opportunity to come knocking at the door or sit and think about something (to attract it) and wait for the phone to ring bringing it to us. I am pretty sure none of us really believe this is going to happen but I also believe some have convinced themselves that luck and fate and other nonsense can bring opportunities into their lives.

What I have found to be true and prefer to believe is that the more you look for opportunities the more you find them. You see, they are always there, you just don't notice and then when you do notice you start believing you attracted them or luck brought them to you.

No matter how you believe your world works, I can promise you that if you spend more time looking for the opportunities listed on the following pages you will not only find them but you will begin to see that opportunities are around you all the time, you just need to pay attention and take action.

You can go through these opportunities one at a time, beginning to end, or search for one that feels right to you or do the "flip of a coin" routine and simply turn to a page and see what opportunity you find.

However you do it, if you take the time to examine a single opportunity and then look for a way to implement it in your life you will soon find it easier and easier to create new and exciting opportunities and live a more fulfilling life and it will all come about without fate, luck, chance or some mystical law of attraction. It will happen because you took the time to seek out and take advantage of an opportunity.

With Aloha
~Larry Czerwonka
February 2012
Hilo Hawaii

#1 Never pass up an opportunity to say something **KIND** behind someone's back :)

We all have sat and listened as someone we know complained about someone else we know, telling us what they did wrong or what they said or some other non- flattering tidbit. What I suggest we try doing more of is spreading "gossip" about the wonderful things that someone has done, how they helped you out or the great project they just created or how they are always helping out down at the library.

We all know people who are doing good things we just never "gossip" about them and I say it's time we started. Spread the rumor about how great the principal at your child's school is because she greets the kids as they come to school each day, or how your wonderful neighbor always smiles and says "Hello" or how your dear friend just finished taking night classes for two years after work and got that degree she was always after.

Look for all the good going on around you and tell others about it. Spread the truth about the good things you have had the privilege of seeing in others.

Start a new fad of good gossip!

#2   Never pass up an opportunity to **LISTEN**, to tune everything else out and just listen to what someone else is saying

This can be a hard one, it's almost not natural but it can be truly amazing.   Listen, I mean really listen, don't let your mind wander to what you want to say when the person talking takes a breath, become absorbed in their every word and their body language, lose yourself in the moment as if your very future depended on your ability to recall exactly what you heard them say, how they said it and how it made you feel.

Listen as if they were giving you some secret recipe for life. Try to not only hear their words but feel their emotions. Be in the now 100%. The better you listen the more likely others are to listen to what you have to say later on and the more likely you are to hear what could be opportunities for you in what they are saying.

The more we pay attention the more opportunities we see and the more we realize that there are infinite opportunities around us all the time, we are just too lost in the past, or dreaming about the future, to see them and then on the rare occasions that we do see them we call it luck or assume we somehow attracted them to us.   But in reality they were there all the time, we were just too busy to notice.

Start being the best listener ever!

#3 Never pass up an opportunity to send a **HAND WRITTEN** note of thanks to someone

All I can say is do this. Do it at least twice a month. Take the time to let someone know they did something that made you take notice. Do it immediately after the event occurred, the next few days at the latest.

There is nothing more heartwarming than getting a note in the mail thanking you for something you have done and nothing drives home just how special it was like a hand written note.

Thank the teacher for the job she did with your child. Thank the postal worker for always having a smile when she delivers your mail. Thank the person that helped you at work. Thank the people on your local neighborhood committee for giving their time to keep the neighborhood safe and maintained.

If you look around there are plenty of opportunities to thank the people in your life for what they are doing. Make it a habit to make the time to send out thank you notes on a regular basis.

Start a tradition of sending thank you notes at least twice a month!

#4   Never pass up an opportunity to **CHALLENGE** the status quo

Status quo is just another word for mediocre. It is the level where all things are equal. It is the easy road that most people travel down. It is not where great ideas come from or fulfilling lives are lived. It is almost like giving up.

The more often that you look for opportunities to break free of the "same as always" ailment, the more fulfilling your life will be.

Doing what everyone else is doing is safe but rarely is it fun or exciting. Doing something for the first time or doing it in a new and unique way is much more rewarding.

Start inventing ways to thrive outside the status quo!

#5   Never pass up an opportunity to **FREE** yourself from a bad habit

We all have things we do that we wish we did not do. It could be as simple as forgetting people's names to something more serious such as smoking or drinking too much.

Whatever the bad habit may be, you should always be on the lookout for something that can act as the catalyst to make you quit doing it. Reading about an accident in which a teenager's life was cut short due to drinking and driving might be what it takes to get you to stop your excessive drinking or hearing about someone losing their job due to always coming in late may make you realize your habit of always being late needs to be rectified. The key is to be watching for the opportunity to find an event that is strong enough to make you finally step up to the plate and eliminate the bad habit from your life.

You will never regret losing a bad habit but you will always be dogged by feelings of guilt as long as the bad habit is still in your life.

Start looking for excuses to stop your bad habit today!

#6   Never pass up an opportunity to **GIVE** to others ... even in small ways

Often we forget that money is not always what people need. There are times when a simple hug might be worth a million dollars to someone who is feeling depressed. Your phone call wishing an old friend a happy birthday may be a lifesaver and those DVD's you no longer watch might do a world of good at the senior center. Stop thinking that you have to give big to help others and start looking for the little things that you can do: shoveling snow from your elderly neighbor's sidewalk; putting your neighbors empty trash cans back into their yard before the wind blows them down the street; giving a few canned goods to the local food bank. Small things truly can go a long way.

Start a monthly routine of going through your house and giving away at least one thing that you no longer use!

#7   Never pass up an opportunity to be **GRATEFUL** for all that you have

Every night before you go off to bed, take a look around you, see what you have and realize how blessed you are to have it. Never take for granted anything that you have because reality is that in an instant (a fire, a flood, an unexpected loss in income) it could all be gone. And should you think you do not have much, simply remember that over one billion people around the world live on less than $4.00 a day and would consider what you have to be living in luxury.

If you have a safe place to sleep at night protected from the elements, if you had a warm meal, if you have clean clothes and shoes to wear, you have more than enough for which to be grateful.

Start each day and end each day being grateful for what you have in your life!

#8   Never pass up an opportunity to **TAKE CARE** of your physical, mental, and emotional well being

What we eat, or more importantly what we choose not to eat or drink is a daily opportunity to choose to be healthy and full of energy, or not. We all know how little we can accomplish when we have a cold and those of us with more than forty years of living behind us know what it's like to wish we had the energy of a ten year old again. The daily opportunity is to move, to keep active, and to eat in ways that ensure we will feel good tomorrow.

Instead of fighting off a cold look for opportunities to not get sick to begin with, learn to eat better, to stay active, to get plenty of rest, and to stress less over life.

Few of the things that we worry about ever come to be so it is better to not worry, to not stress, to keep your mind and body in balance and thereby give yourself a longer and more enjoyable life.

Start treating your body like the sacred vessel that it is!

#9   Never pass up an opportunity to turn someone you just met from a stranger into a **FRIEND**

We rarely think about it but at one time or another everyone in our life was once a stranger. You did not know they even existed, let alone rely on them for advice or share smiles and spend time with them.

The best way to turn a stranger into a friend is to spend just a few minutes with them doing a little exercise a good friend of mine, Grif Frost, taught me called "Born, Raised". Ask the stranger to tell you where they were born, where they grew up, what schools they went to, what childhood memories are vivid in their mind, what they have done and currently do for a living, what hobbies they have. Doing this simple exercise will quickly connect you at a level that normally can take years to establish and turn, what just moments ago was a stranger, into a lifelong friend. No matter what anyone says you can never have too many friends especially ones that are out there rooting for your success.

Stop seeing strangers, start seeing friends!

#10 Never pass up an opportunity to do what you are **AFRAID** to do

Most of us have things that we would rather not do, things that we "fear." For many people it's speaking in front of a group (something that I happen to love to do but it was not always that way I had to make myself do it until it become second nature) or taking a test. The more often you do things you'd rather not do, things that give you butterflies inside, the higher your confidence rises and that rise will open more doors and give you access to more opportunities than ever before. You see, when people around you feel your confidence they conspire (knowingly or not) to help you succeed.

No one likes helping someone that is not willing or is afraid to help themselves. So the simple act of doing things that make you uncomfortable will expand your possibilities and open up new opportunities for you.

Start listing things that you are afraid of and then one by one do them!

#11   Never pass up an opportunity to leave someone's day **BETTER** off than you found it

This is so simple and makes such a huge difference in people's lives. Anytime you go to a friend's house or talk to a co-worker at their desk or simply pay for goods at a check-out counter you have an opportunity to be a ray of sunshine in what may be an otherwise gloomy day.

Words of encouragement go a long way as well as heartfelt praise for things you know someone did. Taking an opportunity to thank someone for being in your life no matter if all they did was ring up your groceries is a cue to smile, to say a few kind words, and to simply acknowledge another human being.

But never be the downer, the friend that points out what's wrong or why things will not work out. Why even go there? After all what is gained by raining on someone's parade?

Focus on, bring up, and point out the good in a friend's life. Raise them up. Leave the room with the friend or stranger wishing you could stay longer and yearning for your next meeting. And thank you, Loren Lilly, for reminding me about this opportunity.

Start making it a habit to acknowledge the people you come into contact with each and every day!

#12 Never pass up an opportunity to let someone else go FIRST

People like to be noticed and letting someone go in front of you or letting them have first pick shows them that you appreciate and "notice" them. It is not a sign of weakness to let someone go ahead of you, in fact it's actually just the opposite. The person that enters a room last actually is the person with the most confidence and maybe the most manners.

Anytime you are approaching a door look around, is there someone just a few steps behind you? Could you open the door and let them go first? Might your simple act be the bright spot in their day?

Start making it a habit to let others go first!

#13 Never pass up an opportunity to do/be **DIFFERENT** for it just might be the difference that changes the world!

Being the same might be easy but it will not change things or solve big problems. Now this does not mean pointing out what you disagree with all the time or putting down what others are doing or what commonly would be referred to as "rocking the boat."

Being different is not about putting others down or "dogging" on what others are doing, it is about doing things your way and letting your success and actions speak for themselves. In fact, as Thumper says, "if you can't say something nice, don't say nothin' at all."

You should even try being different from yourself and see what you discover. If you always do something the same way, if you always take the same route from your house to the store, if you always watch the same shows on TV and listen to the same station on the radio you are limiting your possibilities. Try a new route to work and a new restaurant or start parking blocks away from your destination and walk there and see what new things you discover.

The more you change things, the more you read and listen to different points of view, the more opportunities you will expose yourself to, and the better your chances of coming up with amazing ideas and solutions to everyday and possibly even societal problems. When you look at life from a different point of view you never know just what you will find.

Start forcing new routines into your life. Why not start with changing the hand you use to brush your teeth!

#14 Never pass up an opportunity to be someone's **RAINBOW** when they are feeling down

When someone is feeling down, when they feel storm clouds surrounding them, you have the opportunity to be a rainbow, to remind them that all storms pass. You do this by being arms that hug or a shoulder to lean on or an ear that listens while lips sit by in silence. But most of all you become the rainbow by reminding them that no matter what they are experiencing today, no matter how down they feel, there are always good times just around the corner.

Start being a positive spark in the lives of those around you!

#15 Never pass up an opportunity to **PLAN** before you act

This does not mean days and weeks of planning to the point of not doing any actual work. It does mean thinking through your actions beforehand. Visualize yourself doing the act and seeing the results you'll get. There is nothing more powerful than writing down the steps you will take to achieve a goal, thinking them through and then actually doing them.

You might also find it valuable to state your plan aloud while walking around inside the house. Yes, this might seem strange at first but having a plan, vocalizing that plan, and visualizing the end result that you want is an almost guaranteed way to make it so.

Start creating the habit of doing a little planning before starting any new project!

#16 Never pass up an opportunity to **LEARN** a new skill

Each new skill not only brings new ways of problem solving into your arsenal of talents, it also creates new connections and pathways in your brain which makes coming up with unique ideas next time even easier to do.

A person who can both design and build a house will design a better home than a person who merely designs but has no clue how to build or a person who builds but has no idea how to design.

Every new skill also raises your self-confidence and makes you more likely to succeed at all that you attempt.

Start learning a new skill at least four times a year!

#17   Never pass up an opportunity to find silence and let your **CREATIVITY** come forth in abundance

Silence is a huge advantage that our forefathers had over us and why I think many of them came up with so many inventions and works of art in such short lifetimes. Because only when you are not being bombarded with outside stimulus can you focus on a problem and find unique, creative, and powerful solutions.

This blocking out of the noise is why so many people get ideas while in the shower, it's not silent there but when the only sound is that of water spraying through the air, when there are no other distractions, it frees the brain from working so hard to manage what's happening around us and lets it focus in on problems. Try it.

Finding at least fifteen minutes a day to sit in silence could be a life changer and unlock the creative genius that lives hidden behind the chaos of your daily life.

Start making time each day for silence!

#18   Never pass up an opportunity to help others to **SUCCEED**

Success of those around you does not mean you cannot succeed too. In fact, it is said that you can only be as successful as the five people you interact with the most in life. So, helping those close to you reach their goals and encouraging them to shoot for the stars improves your chances of success as well.

Often all it takes to help someone else succeed is to encourage them in their endeavors and telling other people about the great things your friends are doing. Or, it may also involve you introducing one friend to another. You will only know what you can do to help others by asking them what they are trying to do, what goals they are trying to achieve.

One note of caution, when offering your help to people who have not known you for very long expect them to be leery of your motives. After all, they have been trained by society to be wary of strangers bearing gifts or in this case offering a helping hand. Now I have found you can quickly quell these fears by explaining your motives up front. Tell them the more everyone around you succeeds the better your chances for success and the better off your entire community will be.

Start asking your friends their goals and then look for ways to help them get there!

#19 Never pass up an opportunity to turn a frown into a SMILE

No one wakes up hoping to have a bad day, stuff just happens and we react to it negatively and the next thing you know we are wearing a frown. But there is always a smile waiting to come out, it just needs some encouragement. Remember this next time you see someone wearing a frown.

A simple smile, a reassuring nod, a look that says "I see you" may be enough to turn a frown around and bring a little rush of goodwill to someone's day. Life happens but nothing turns a frown around faster than knowing that someone else cares.

Start doing all that you can to become a slayer of frowns!

#20   Never pass up an opportunity to take a day off and **RECHARGE**, especially if you can do it outdoors!

There is a reason that no professional sports have their players competing in a game day in and day out. Without breaks between games players would burn out, would suffer more injuries, and would never have time to practice and get better. No matter how much we love what we do and how many hours we think we must work, the reality is that the more opportunities we take to not be buried in our work, the more we seek out and find an hour or two each week to let ourselves recharge the better we will perform.

You cannot give 100% week-in and week-out, you need time away from work to recharge. In fact pushing yourself to get work done for an extended period of time will actually produce less and at a lesser quality than if you cut back and spent a little more time away from the rush of needing to always be in production mode. Now, the best way to recharge is to get outside, go to a park, soak in the beauty of nature, take deep breaths and let your mind be free from deadlines and the office for a change.

Start setting aside a few hours every week to get away from the job and out in nature!

#21 Never pass up an opportunity to **HELP** someone else step into the spotlight

Often we don't even think about it, but if you happen to be in a position where others listen to what you have to say or clamor to purchase your goods or services, then you are in a position to allow someone else the experience of being in the spotlight every now and then.

Talking up the great job someone else is doing or asking someone to present their idea at the next meeting or making the community aware of the talents of a friend or co-worker with a letter to the editor, all of these things which may seem trivial to you could be the highlight of the month (or even the year) for the person you shine the light on. It might embarrass a person or two when you single them out but it will also make them feel good inside knowing that you took the time to point out to others the qualities you see in them or in what they have accomplished.

Start shining a spotlight on the talent you see around you!

#22 Never pass up an opportunity to **IMPROVE** yourself

We can always find things to get better at. There is always something we do or don't do that can be improved. This can range from something simple like making a better omelet to things that are a little more difficult such as complaining less or not jumping to conclusions.

The key is to be observant of what you are doing or what you are about to say and ask yourself if you could do it better. It can also mean trying to use your left hand more (if you happen to be right handed) or being on time for appointments or taking a little extra time to review your work before handing it in.

Even mundane tasks such as washing the dishes or mowing the lawn can be improved upon. If a task is worth doing, it's worth doing better than you did it last time. You should focus and give each task your all and become the best dish washer, gardener, listener, or friend that you can be.

Start working to be better today than you were yesterday!

#23 Never pass up an opportunity to leave a place **BETTER OFF** than you found it

Chairs left sitting away from the table, litter in the park, an item in the grocery store sitting on the floor, there are always things that can be picked up, put up, or straightened up to make where you just were better off than how it was when you arrived. Looking for these things not only allows you to do a "good deed," which often makes you feel better, but it also keeps you connected to the moment which is the only place where life can be truly lived.

Start looking for ways to "tidy up" your surroundings!

#24 Never pass up an opportunity to **SPEND TIME** with family and friends

Believe it or not there will come a day when that family member or friend is no longer there and it is impossible to spend time with them. So stop being too busy to go for a walk, or to meet friends for dinner, or to watch a movie, or to play a game with family members because you never know when this time may be the last time.

The more time you make to enjoy family and friends the better the memories you will have to look back on in the future, comforted in the knowledge that you made the time to be with them. Make it to their play. Be there to see them get an award. Make time to talk story on the lanai.

Start finding ways to spend more time with the people you love!

#25 Never pass up an opportunity to **TRY SOMETHING** you have never done before

Doing something new is scary but it also is what keeps us alive. It wakes us up. It challenges us. It keeps our brain working. No, you will not do it perfect the first time and you might even look foolish trying but it is better to have tried it, even if you find you don't want to do it again, than to be sitting in your rocking chair when you are 80 wishing you had tried it when you had a chance and wondering what it would have been like to see that city or build that boat or having played that game or written that novel.

The more things you try, the more you challenge yourself, the more self-confidence you will have and the more successful your life will be and the less likely you are to have a "mid-life crisis."

Start making it a habit to try something new at least once a month!

#26   Never pass up an opportunity to grow a **SMILE** on someone's face :)

The simple act of smiling at someone, even someone you do not know, can bring a smile to their face and for all you know it may be the only smile they see all day. A smile and a nod that says "I see you and I am glad that I see you" does not cost a thing so why not give smiles away as often as you can each day?

Besides, the more you acknowledge others the better you will feel inside and who knows that simple smile or nod of the head might be the opening to a beautiful friendship.

Start smiling more at everyone you see each day!

#27 Never pass up an opportunity to **ENCOURAGE** someone to pursue their dreams

No matter how "impossible" someone's dream may sound to you, encourage them to pursue it. Nothing great was ever the result of a ho-hum dream. No one ever created without first having a dream and the desire to bring it to life. Cars, satellites, the television, even the printed book were all impossible dreams at one time or another that eventually were realized by someone. Why, even Disneyland was once an impossible dream, same with the Harry Potter novels, or Star Wars.

Be the YES in the room when you hear someone tell you their goals.

Be the cheerleader, encouraging others in the pursuit of their dreams.

Stop making that "it will never happen face" when you hear someone else's dream and begin instead to light up with enthusiasm at the mere thought of their dream coming true!

Start asking everyone about their dreams and then look for opportunities to help them make their dreams come true.

#28   Never pass up an opportunity to have a **GOOD TIME!**

Having a good time is a choice. If you don't think it is, watch any sporting event. In the stands are two groups of people watching the same game yet one group leaves thrilled and the other leaves with frowns on their face and even tears in their eyes. How can that be? They all saw the same game yet the simple act of making an emotional attachment to the game's outcome affected their mood. They can only be "happy" if their team wins. The game itself, the good plays, the effort, the athleticism, the excitement of being in the stands, none of that matter if all they focus on is the final score.

Every day is just like the game, you choose to find what you enjoy and focus on it and have a great day or you zoom in on what you dislike and ruin your day.

It really is a choice and you make it, constantly, minute by minute each and every day, so why not choose to have a good time?

Start paying more attention to what you like each day!

#29 Never pass up an opportunity to be curious, excited and **ENGAGED** with life

I love where I live because should I somehow get complacent about life all I have to do is go downtown and watch the tourists clicking pictures, pointing, smiling, and enjoying all that they are seeing around them to remind me how special it all is.

Take time every day and really look at all that is around you, from nature to the man-made, with the wonderment of seeing it for the very first time and enjoying its splendor. Marvel at what the person who made it must have gone through to arrange all the pieces in just such a manner that it now exists in that form. It all is so amazing if you stop and think about it.

Start looking at your surroundings like a tourist who has saved for years to be standing right where you are today. Be in awe of what surrounds you.

#30 Never pass up an opportunity to start a NEW
TRADITION

Believe it or not at one time or another every single tradition that you celebrate did not exist. Makes you think.

In my case the understanding that every tradition was "created" gave me permission to create my own traditions, be it as simple as taking my grandson to the park to feed the ducks on the 2nd Saturday of every month or having a celebration of "just because" with my wife on October the 2nd of every year.

There really are no rules, no limits, you can create whatever tradition you want; just follow through and do it and make it fun. But also be willing to change it and replace it with an even better tradition.

The key is to stop waiting for someone else's tradition to tell you when to send flowers to someone you love or spend some time with family and friends.

I told my wife years ago we could celebrate valentine's day and birthdays and mother's day or we could celebrate throughout the year whenever we felt like it but we would not do both. She chose random celebrations on the spur of the moment (which is now our tradition: don't wait for "special days" to buy a gift or send flowers or go out to dinner, do it when the mood strikes) over the status quo celebrations.

Start one new tradition this year. Make it fun and memorable!

#31 Never pass up an opportunity to **LEARN** to say 'hello,' 'thank you' and 'pardon me' in another language

Even if you cannot speak more than these three simple phrases it will go a long way to making you welcome in a foreign country and might even entice you to explore even more of the local language.

Yes, a smile is the same in all languages, but a smile followed by thank you in the proper language goes even farther!

Start learning how to say these phrases in the local language before your next trip abroad.

#32 Never pass up an opportunity to create **PEACE** in your life

For me, peace is a lack of stress. You see, stress is the biggest killer that there is. The way to relive stress is to take a few deep breaths and to look for the things around you that you enjoy and stay focused on them.

If there is someone in your life that upsets you either remove them or remove yourself from their presence. It might be hard but it must be done.

And stop worrying because worry is a waste of your imagination and beside, ever notice how rare it is that predictions of doom and gloom come to pass?

Don't worry, be happy ... it really does work!

#33 Never pass up an opportunity to weave something **NEW** into the tapestry of your life

As a child we delighted in new things. We even got excited when we took hold of a crayon and ran it across a piece of paper and saw the trail it left behind. We should always be looking for new things, be they as simple as a new way to drive to your favorite spot downtown, to finding a new radio program to listen to, or to a better way for growing herbs. The key is to always learn new techniques which not only gives you more self-confidence but also more tools to draw on when you encounter a "problem."

If the only way you know to fix something that is broke is by using duct tape you will have limited the possible outcomes, whereas if you know how to use glue or to weld or how to create a tongue and grove joint you are much more likely to find a more fitting solution for fixing what is broke. So when you see someone doing something new take notice, ask questions, and learn to do it too. Discover how to use a vang or normalize data or anything else that will add to your knowledge and give you more ways to approach anything that might come your way.

Start exploring new fields of endeavor and learning how craftsmen in that field go about their work.

#34 Never pass up an opportunity to live by the words you **SPEAK**

One of the best compliments ever paid me was that I am "all walk and no talk," meaning I do it rather than spending a lot of time talking about it. Now that was not always the case, it has taken years to walk more and talk less or to talk and then make sure I followed it up with actions. And there still are times when my talking gets ahead of my walking.

I have found that the best way to make sure you follow talk up with actions is to tell as many people as you can what you plan on doing. At first people will think you are just dreaming or bragging but over time, as they see you back up what you say with actions, they will not only believe you will do what you say but will also offer to help to "make it so."

Having a handful of people that you know are waiting to see if you follow through or not is a very good motivator for getting things done.

If need be write down things that you have said and then review that list from time to time to see if you followed through or not. If not, then you need to consider saying less or stepping up to the plate and following through with actions.

Start right now by writing down what you plan to do in the next 30 days and then DO IT!

#35 Never pass up an opportunity to **REINVENT** your life

The reason for re-inventing is to condition yourself to enjoy change, to keep from becoming a creature of habit for habit does not lead to evolution. If you still wrote like you did when you were seven or crossed the street with the confidence of a three year old your life would be scary. By doing new things, by becoming the 6 A.M. neighborhood walker and then the 6 A.M. writer and then the 6 A.M. swimmer and then the 6 A.M. web surfer, you open your life to more opportunities and keep from getting stuck in a rut.

A routine is good for machines and factory production but is ruinous as a way to live a life.

Re-inventing is the key to a more bountiful tomorrow.

Start mixing up when and how you do things and see how eye opening it can be.

#36 Never pass up an opportunity to ask yourself "**WHAT** am I trying to do with my life?"

When was the last time you sat down and thought about what you hope to accomplish in your lifetime? Have you ever even done it?

Too many people are just trying to get through the day, to think about such a grand idea and that is a very sad use of the miracle of life that has been granted us.

We should all be trying to do something amazing, something that at the very least inspires others to have a purpose for their lives. Something that lasts beyond our lifetime. Something that shows we were here and that we understood the value of this gift of life and the need to give back in some way.

You should look at what you are trying to become at least twice a year ... What do you want people to remember you for?

Start making it a habit to question what you are doing with your life and why you are doing it, at least twice a year.

#37 Never pass up an opportunity to keep **MOVING** forward

We often find ourselves stationary as if we have forgotten where we are heading and find it much simpler to just sit and let life go by.

Why is that? Could it be because stopping is just so easy? After all, you can't run into any roadblocks when you are not moving.

Imagine that you are driving from the west coast to the east coast and that you really, really want to make the trip. Now as long as you keep your final destination in mind, the occasional flat tire or the engine trouble will only slow you down for the amount of time it takes to get them fixed. But the key is keeping that final destination in mind at all times and never letting a small bump in the road stop you.

Too often something as insignificant as a broken wiper blade is enough of an excuse for us to stop. Don't let that happen to you. Don't let the allure of an excuse stop you from your destination. Forge ahead with all your might. Never forget why you started on the journey in the first place.

Start looking for reasons to keep moving toward your destination as opposed to excuses for giving up.

#38 Never pass up an opportunity to be **OVER THE TOP**

Elvis, KISS, Lady Gaga, Liberace they all have known that the way to be noticed, the way to make things happen, the way to attract people to want to work with you is to be "out there!" The timid person that sits in the back and watches will never have their phone ring off the hook with offers of any kind. But the person that stands up, that does even the simplest of tasks with enough flair to make it memorable will find it much easier to find work or help or whatever it is they are seeking in life.

Stop being the "wall-flower." Start being noticed!

#39 Never pass up an opportunity to **ASSOCIATE** yourself with passionate and caring people

The people that you associate with on a daily basis have a large impact on your life, maybe even more than you realize. If you surround yourself with people who are constantly giving back to the community and are passionate about their work you cannot help but feel energized by them and inspired by them to do great things with your life.

If all your friends spend Friday night watching TV or at the bar, then more than likely that is what you will do too. But if your friends spend the night helping out at the soup kitchen or at the art gallery or working late on an amazing project then you will be more likely to be doing those things too.

The people in your life are a reflection of where you are going and what you are doing.

Start spending more time with people that are actively creating life as opposed to ones that are sitting on the sidelines watching life pass by

#40 Never pass up an opportunity to associate yourself with slightly **CRAZY** people

Groundbreaking ideas rarely come from the "normal" channels. Great advances in any field usually come from or are influenced by the people that live on the fringes. The more varied the people you associate with, the wider the cultural voices in your life, the greater your chance of coming up with truly innovative and successful solutions to the problems you encounter.

The guy that's always wearing the purple hat or roller skating in the park, why even the person who really believes in conspiracy theories, they all have a point of view to offer that actually makes your life richer and gives you more options with which to address any problems that arise in your work place or your private life.

Stop pushing people away because their ideas do not line up with yours. There are gems of insight to be gained by listening to "crazy" ideas.

#41 Never pass up an opportunity to get off the beaten path and **EXPLORE** the road less traveled

Going it alone, taking off on an uncharted course might be scary but it is so rewarding. Being the first to try something, to see something, to experience what others can only imagine, not only makes life more enjoyable, it also opens your life to a wide variety of possibilities.

What's the fun in doing something just like 10,000 people did it before you? Worse, what's to be gained by doing something just like everyone else has done before, knowing that at the end of the day everyone will still complain about the results, because the tried-and-true way of doing things has never led to a solution: think war on drugs; or measures to end poverty; or a better way of teaching.

Yes, it's what has always been done and it has the same known downfalls but, don't be afraid of taking a risk on something new. Too many firms have a culture where new is bad and only doing what has been done before is acceptable. This may have its place but taking the new route and seeing what new results can be found is much more rewarding and is the only way to find solutions to age old problems.

Start poking and exploring in the places where the path is less well defined.

#42 Never pass up an opportunity to **CHANGE** the question

Often we cannot find the solution to a problem simply because we are asking the wrong questions. We get so stuck in the way we word the problem that we make it next to impossible to come up with a solution.   By changing the question we open up whole new possibilities. For example, if we change the question from "how do we build more jails to handle prison overcrowding" to "how do we make it so we only need one jail?" The change in the question sets our minds off on new routes and new possibilities that the original question never made possible.

Next time you are stuck for a solution, try changing how you state the problem.

#43 Never pass up an opportunity to see someone not as they are today but as what they might **BECOME**

Most of us smile when we see children and find it easy to imagine the great things they will do with their lives but once a person reaches their mid-twenties we, for some unknown reason, begin to stop seeing a person's future as something great because we get stuck on their history. We forget that everyone can change (if they really, really want to) and that the change can be huge. We limit their future to the path that has been their past, as if the wake behind a boat determined where the boat could go next.

The more we look not at what people are today but instead imagine what they can truly become, the more we help others live the life of their dreams and maybe, just maybe,   it will be our encouragement that helps them get to their potential.

Ask people where they are heading, what their goals and dreams are and then not only see them accomplishing it but also encourage them to make sure they get there. If it helps try imagining that they are five again and just starting their dream, would you tell a child that they cannot be a doctor? Then why do you limit the future of a twenty-five year old?

Start believing in the potential that lies within us all.

#44 Never pass up an opportunity to step back and **APPRECIATE** what you just created

We rush around so much at times that we forget to take a minute and truly appreciate what we just did. And this applies to everything we do. Have you ever looked at the lawn you just mowed or the tire you just changed or the painting you just finished and truly thought how amazing it is?

Everything that you do is amazing and deserves a minute of appreciation. This pause is the only way to not get stuck in the fast lane where you are always thinking about what's next instead of taking a moment to appreciate what you have just done.

Start making it a habit to pause, even for just a second, and appreciate every task, no matter the size, as you complete it.

#45 Never pass up an opportunity to remain **FOCUSED** on your destination

If you were driving from Los Angeles to New York you would always know, throughout the trip, your final destination. You could look at a map and see just how far you had come and how far was left to go and if there were any interesting stops you might like to make along the way. You need to do the same with your life. You need to have a destination and remind yourself where you are headed and what route you are taking to get there.

In fact, another sure way to stay on track is to tell as many supportive people as you can where you are headed, since they will occasionally and often unexpectedly ask how you are doing, are you still on course? did you get there yet?

The more often you remind yourself where you are going the greater the chance that you will arrive.

Start checking at least once a month to make sure you are still heading in the proper direction and getting closer to your destination.

#46 Never pass up an opportunity to speak enthusiastically, to motivate and **INSPIRE** others

Never be the naysayer in the room, the person pointing out all that you don't like or how the proposal will never work. Learn to speak about all the good you see around you and about how wonderful tomorrow will be. People will enjoy being around you and sharing with you and more importantly, will be there to help you.

When someone tells you their dreams, focus on the way you see their dream will come true and talk about that, not the obstacles (or obstacle illusions) that you imagine. By doing this, eventually, you will stop seeing obstacle illusions and it will become "habit" to raise up others and their dreams as well as speak about a bright future and a better tomorrow, for no matter how wonderful today may be, tomorrow should always be seen as even better.

Start making it a habit to keep quiet when you have nothing positive to say and begin speaking up when you see and hear things that you like.

#47 Never pass up an opportunity to **GET ALONG** with others

This can be hard, but is oh so rewarding and exposes you to a wide variety of views and ideas which you might otherwise have never known existed. The key to getting along is to focus on the areas where you agree with others and to spend less time and emotion where you disagree.

Remind yourself that arguing never changes beliefs, but actions, over time, can slowly wear away the most stubborn of beliefs. Spend time and energy on your actions, focus on what others are saying that you agree with and never lose sight of the fact that getting along and being more judicious with your words is not a sign of weakness or giving in. In fact, it shows that you are coming from a place of power and are confident in your own views.

The person that argues and yells and resorts to name calling is not passionate about their views, they actually are very insecure and think somehow that by berating others they can be "right." Listening to others and letting them have their say and not arguing is a good thing and will help you better understand how someone else sees the world.

Stop looking for arguments. Start being more compassionate.

#48 Never pass up an opportunity to help a caterpillar become a **BUTTERFLY**

Everyone is a caterpillar until they start doing something that they feel gives them life. For natures caterpillar the change into a butterfly is pre-destined. For most of us however, doing what we are passionate about takes courage and effort.

More people will tell us why we cannot become butterflies than those who encourage us to do what we really want.

Always be the voice of encouragement telling folks they can leave their caterpillar life and fly like a butterfly, it just takes effort and time. In fact, even "bug" them to spend some time really focusing on what they really want (like the time a caterpillar spends in the cocoon) and then help them to break out and pursue their passion.

Start looking for people in your life that are still caterpillars but seem ready to put forth the effort necessary to transform into a magnificent butterfly and give them all the help and encouragement that you can.

#49 Never pass up an opportunity to Picture Your **SUCCESS**

There is one thing that is more powerful than writing down your goals and that is seeing you goals accomplished in your mind. Seeing a successful future, where your goals are obtained, is a powerful motivator for keeping you on track and working through obstacles on the way to your goal.

Visualization can also help with a new task or a job interview or even a presentation you have to give. See yourself successfully performing the task over and over in your head. This visualization will make it easier to be successful when the time comes to perform.

Athletes do this all the time with great success. They see themselves scoring goals or getting a clutch hit or making a diving save. To the mind there is little difference between actually performing a task and visualizing it. There is no easier way to "practice" success. Visualizing your success also lowers the chances you will spend time worrying about a less than desirable outcome.

Start learning to see each task completed in your mind before you start to work on it.

#50 Never pass up an opportunity to **DO THINGS** that blow people away in their scope and uniqueness

Doing things just like everyone else does them might be enough to get the job done but will it make others take notice or lead to more opportunities? If Elvis had just stood and sang like the other singers of his day he would not have been the huge celebrity that he was. Yes, he had a great voice but it was the little extra twist that made him unique and got him noticed.

Anything worth doing is worth doing with a little extra so people pay more attention. Doing just a little extra in a unique way will set you apart from everyone else and lead to even more opportunities in your life. Why be the crossing guard when you can be the crossing guard that waves at all the cars and runs off the street after the last child has left the roadway.

Start adding just a little extra to the things that you do.

#51 Never pass up an opportunity to **DO THINGS** that inspire others

Yes we all do things to make a living but how often does what we do inspire others? Simple things like picking up trash while you are walking through the park can inspire those around you. Things that may seem insignificant could actually inspire others to do more, such as always being on time for meetings, always having good manners, always tipping the cab driver or the waiter. Giving your time to help at the food bank or at a community event are also good ways to inspire others to become more involved and give back.

Start living an inspired life and by so doing inspire others to join you.

ABOUT THE AUTHOR

Larry Czerwonka lives in Hilo Hawaii with his wife of 30 years Diane. Larry's passion for solving difficult problems and helping others led to the founding of the Big Island Empowerment Network in 2009. Members from all walks of life come together once a month for an "Idea Exchange" where sharing, caring, and making things happen are always the focus. In 2011 Larry put together TEDxWaiakea **www.tedxwaiakea.com** which brought unique ideas and solutions to Hilo Town. He also spoke at the event and talked about "Game Day" which is a unique way for running any business.

Larry helps businesses and people move from average to amazing and currently is working on a project to change how communities function.

You can read more of Larry's ideas at **www.happinessu.org/tc**
And see all of Larry's books at **www.happinessu.org/books**
You can connect with Larry at **www.twitter.com/#!/larryczerwonka**
and at **www.facebook.com/larry.czerwonka**

Made in the USA
Charleston, SC
10 May 2012